THE COLOR WAS BLACK:
A RACE ATTACK

By Bishop E. Bernard Jordan

ISBN 0-939241-06-4

His Color Was Black - A Race Attack

2nd Printing

Copyright © 1996 by Bishop E. Bernard Jordan, Zoe Ministries, Church Street Station, P.O. Box 270, New York, NY 10008-0270. All rights reserved. No part of this book may be reproduced in any form without written permission from the author. Printed in the United States of America. Unless otherwise noted, all Scriptures are taken from the King James version of the Holy Bible.

DEDICATION

This book is dedicated to my oldest daughter
Naomi Deborah Jordan, who will carry the Word of the Lord,
boldly proclaiming "His Color Was Black."

In Gratitude

We'd like to give the following individuals a special thank you for their faithfulness and support in helping to make our dream come true:

Joseph & Comfort Barron
Nancy Beaver
Doreen Bogle
Delilay Braswell
Oswald Brown
Alma Davis
Pastor Richard Eberiga
Eugene Henry
Beatrice C. Hudson
Wynell Johnson
Elder Fitzgerald A. King
Pastor Henderson Maddox
Samuel & Felicia Matthews
Pastor Donnie McIntyre
Pastor Connie Miles
A. Chris Nelms
Claudia D. Palmer
Pastor Sylvester & Evangelist Elizabeth Sanders
Florence F. Smith
Joyce Smith
Jackie Stewart
Tony & Wanda Summers
Alfreda Turner
Reverend Franklin W. Williamson Jr.

Because of their generosity and obedience to the Spirit of God, we know that they have opened the door for miracles, and we believe that He shall cause the gems of wisdom that are contained within these pages to be made manifest in each of their lives, for the reward of the Lord is sure and addeth no sorrow!

In His Love and Service,
Bishop E. Bernard & Pastor Debra Jordan

CONTENTS

1............**CHAPTER ONE**
Undressing The Lie

9............**CHAPTER TWO**
Truth Brings Division

17............**CHAPTER THREE**
In Living Color

25............**CHAPTER FOUR**
The Right Image and Right Message

33............**CHAPTER FIVE**
No Trains to Heaven

43............**CHAPTER SIX**
Lies, Garbage and Trash

57............**CHAPTER SEVEN**
The Liberating Power of the Gospel

PREFACE

WARNING: This message will pierce hearts like a two-edged sword, leaving a bloody trail of decimated false doctrine, error and half-truths. Good! The quicker the surgery the sooner the healing process can begin.

Why is a book like this necessary? Because we bought the lie that Christianity was a white man's religion, which led to many of our people becoming indoctrinated into the muslim religion and culture. Actually, we didn't buy it; it was systematically and freely fed to us over hundreds of years. It became our food. You are what you eat. We became docile "house niggers" afraid to upset the status quo, afraid to embrace the image of God within us and afraid to showcase our blackness!

We gave up our African heritage as kings and queens, and became Americanized mail boys and "girl Fridays." We gave up our dance. We tuned down our music. We gave up our inherent leadership abilities and accepted "pew positions" in white churches. Worse, we gave up Jesus, a black man according to Scripture, for a white man's version of his blond hair, blue-eyed European cousin. And we did it all in the name of Christianity declaring that "color doesn't matter we are all one in Christ Jesus."

Color does matter. If it didn't God would not have meticulously recorded the colors of the priests' garments, the color of the tabernacle furnishings and the color of Jesus' feet!

His Color Was Black: A Race Attack will challenge, inspire, infuriate and alienate -- depending upon your mindset regarding racism in the Church and society at large. No matter how you respond it won't change the fact that His Color Was Black! It's time to face the truth, expel the lie and walk in freedom. Many people accept the Christ of the Spirit, but not Jesus the man. It makes you wonder if they are really born again because "every spirit that confesseth not that Jesus Christ is come in the flesh is not of God." (1 John 4:3)

I encourage you to examine yourself, to see if you are in the faith!

Bishop E. Bernard Jordan

Bishop E. Bernard Jordan

CHAPTER ONE
Undressing the Lie

As he spake these words, many believed on him. Then said Jesus to those Jews which believed on him, If ye continue in my word, then are ye my disciples indeed;
And ye shall know the truth, and the truth shall make you free. They answered him, We be Abraham's seed, and were never in bondage to any man: how sayest thou, Ye shall be made free? Jesus answered them, Verily, verily, I say unto you, Whosoever committeth sin is the servant of sin.
And the servant abideth not in the house forever: but the Son abideth forever.
If the Son therefore shall make you free, ye shall be free indeed. I know that ye are Abraham's seed; but ye seek to kill me, because my word hath no place in you. I speak that which I have seen with my Father: and ye do that which ye have seen with your father.
They answered and said unto him, Abraham is our father.

> *Jesus saith unto them, If ye were Abraham's children, ye would do the works of Abraham.*
> *But now ye seek to kill me, a man that hath told you the truth, which I have heard of God: this did not Abraham.*
> *Ye do the deeds of your father. Then said they to him,*
> *We be not born of fornication; we have one Father, even God. Jesus said unto them, If God were your Father, ye would love me: for I proceeded forth and came from God; neither came I of myself, but he sent me.*
>
> John 8:30-42

PROPHETIC PRINCIPLE #1
Truth evokes anger within the people of the lie.

When you begin to tell the Truth, people will seek to kill you. Everyone is not a lover of Truth. Some people accost the Truth and resent its intrusion into the lie that has become the womb of their existence. There are many people who are at war with the Truth. We must also understand that Truth is not a philosophy, but rather, Truth is a Person. Truth is Deity. Truth is the incarnation of Jesus Christ because Jesus lets us know that He is the Way, the Truth and the Life. Truth is a Reality; the Reality of the Person of Jesus Christ.

Jesus, in speaking to this group, encourages them to remain in His Word. We also notice that Jesus positions the challenge to His opponents as an unusual assertion as He connects Truth (Himself) with freedom. When we talk about freedom and liberation, and what it means to be free, Jesus makes it very clear to us that we shall know the Truth and He shall make us free.

Now, I am going to deal with certain areas and issues that are very touchy, especially concerning racism, and oppression. It will become quite painful to a lot of people who would rather not deal with those things. They'd rather that I would talk about heaven or talk about love. They question the necessity of getting involved with "social issues".

A prophet is called and anointed by God to speak concerning hard issues. Oftentimes, when we look at the apparent "glory and glamour" of the prophetic anointing, we like to focus our attention on the blessing of the Lord and on His marvelous works on our behalf. However, as we look at the prophets in the Scriptures, we notice that the prophets were confrontational; they always carried a message aimed at the oppressors of their day. They always pointed their finger at a system of injustice. They stood for true righteousness, which would correct those things that were wrong and declare the illumination of the truth from God's Word. The prophet was in the business of undressing the lie!

PROPHETIC PRINCIPLE #2
Jesus is the Truth!

In John 8:37, Jesus provoked some individuals to the point that they wanted to kill Him because of His stand for the truth. In verse 38, we see the debate concerning fatherhood.

> *"I speak that which I have seen with My Father: and ye do that which you have seen with your father."*

When we begin to behold the oppression and injustice that has permeated today's society, and the remnants of the evils of slavery, we begin to understand that you can discern the father of the individuals who commit such actions. One who is of the seed of Abraham and has God for their Father would not seek to enslave me; rather, they would seek to empower me. They would seek to bring about my freedom and eradicate poverty. One's actions define the paternal genitor; your actions will tell me the father you're seeing.

PROPHETIC PRINCIPLE #3
Truth brings freedom.

We must begin to tell the truth. There have been many individuals who duped us into thinking they were telling the truth, but the message that they brought to us never brought liberation to us as individuals or as a people. Most of us have been in church all of our lives, yet we're still poor and struggling for survival. We've been taught to worship the Lord with the rattling of the chains of captivity as a constant reverberation of the agony that we have been experiencing. We've been to church almost daily; Sunday morning, Sunday evening, Thursday night prayer meeting, Tuesday night Bible Study and Friday night service. We went to church with our mother, our grandmother, our great-grandmother; we wore all white, black and white, choir robes and white gloves...and yet for some strange reason, most of us are still living in a rented situation with bank accounts that are full of zeros.

We must begin to re-examine the gospel. If what we have been taught has not brought us liberation, then it is not the gospel of Jesus Christ! The Apostle Paul knew this truth, which is why he stated "I am not ashamed of the gospel of Jesus Christ, for it is the power of God unto salvation."

When Jesus was confronted by the Jews who disputed what He was teaching, the Jews claimed Abraham for their father. Jesus rejected their claim on the basis of their intent to kill Him. People who declare the truth are always harassed. Jesus stated, in verse 40, "...Now ye seek to kill me, a man that hath told you the truth which I have heard of God; this did not Abraham."

When Abraham heard the truth, he embraced the truth. When satan hears the truth, he will seek to silence the truth. When you begin to walk into the image of God and become what He has desired for you to be; when you walk in truth, and begin to make a qualified decision that you are going to be wealthy and refuse to walk in poverty, you will walk in the awareness that you serve a living, liberating Saviour. When you start to embrace the truth, you will be challenged by an enemy that will be assigned to destroy the truth that is in you. It will try to kill you.

PROPHETIC PRINCIPLE #4
Prophets speak to hard issues.

There are many individuals that will be offended by this message. They will insist that it's not of God. Unfortunately, God has placed a mechanism within us that causes us to become habitual in our behavior. When one sits in darkness for a long time, they will adapt to it. Light becomes painful. Many of us have been shown an image of Jesus that is contrary to the description that is found in the Scriptures. Somebody lied and dressed it up as the truth.

When we are conditioned to walk around planet earth calling certain individuals "massa" that God never designed for us to become subservient to, then there has to come a rude awakening that you have been dwelling in an improper environment. God did not intend for you to go through life with your head hung down, eating the dust of their feet as they ascend the ladder of success. The gospel of Jesus Christ will bring change, and when change comes the system will arise to try to kill the truth that is in you.

When truth comes, they will take your programs away from you. Frankly, programs are crippling. They underscore your dependency upon them. It wasn't any different when the children of Israel were enslaved in Egypt. When truth began to emerge in their midst, the government said "Make brick without straw." The intention of God is for us to walk in covenant with Him. He wants our total dependency to be in Him only, for He is Jehovah Jireh—He is the Lord our Provider. He wants us to walk as Abraham with such a knowledge of God's Presence that we boast with Abraham; "No man has made me rich but Almighty God."

PROPHETIC PRINCIPLE #5
Prophets undress the lies of their day.

> *In the last day, that great day of the feast, Jesus stood and cried, saying, If any man thirst, let him come unto me, and drink.*
> *He that believeth on me, as the scripture hath said, out of his belly shall flow rivers of living water.*
> *(But this spake he of the Spirit, which they that believe on him should receive: for the Holy Ghost was not yet given; because that Jesus was not yet glorified.)*
>
> John 7:37-39

Isn't it interesting that the Holy Ghost was given after Jesus ascended? God knew that we would need a Comforter because of the work which He had set before us! He sent One that would be called alongside to help in our struggle. And He is the Spirit of Truth. The Spirit helps our infirmities.....He strengthens the areas in which you are not firm, and the areas in which you are weak. God is presenting His ability before you to draw upon, saying, "Get off welfare, eliminate government programs, and learn to lean on the Holy Ghost who will give you wisdom and show you the silver and gold!!" I don't know about you, but I'm tired of the crippling effects of the welfare system. A church that is caught in the web of a "welfare mentality," that cannot make a move unless someone is giving them something for free, cannot speak the truth because it is obligatorily bound by its corporate sponsorship. They will have placed their necks in a noose of their own making through the strings of favors that demand to be paid. A puppet cannot speak beyond the mind of its master.

> **PROPHETIC PRINCIPLE #6**
>
> **Prophets are ordained to confront injustice.**

Verses 40-41:
Many of the people therefore, when they heard this saying, said, Of a truth this is the Prophet. Others said, This is the Christ. But some said, Shall Christ come out of Galilee?

God has a way of secretly raising up individuals hidden from the eyes of an evil and oppressive system. The prejudicial system of Jesus' day wished to deny the place of Jesus' origin. The stigma upon Galilee was much like the stigmas that exist in our midst today when one mentions the names of Chicago, New York, Newark...cities whose bones are aching with the pain of an oppressed people within its walls.

CHAPTER 2
Truth Brings Division

The Scripture immortalizes the societal bias by recording the question that someone asked, "Can anything good come out of Nazareth?" Division was present, even in the day of our Lord. His Presence brought Truth, and Truth brings division.

Our phone lines have been extremely busy lately because this current message of Truth is being spoken. The message has provoked more audience response than any other, because Truth brings division. Some accuse me of being a racist, and pronounce that I "am not of God." Some challenge the doctrine. Others yell into the phone and say "You're causing division in the church!" And all that is simply happening is that Truth is being proclaimed...for when Truth shows up, it brings division.

Jesus said, "I come with a sword to put mother against daughter, father against son." When the truth comes, the sword divides asunder. Never underestimate the power of the truth. The truth has a way of provoking the hearts of people and inducing responses which will make you say, "My God, I thought they were saved!" The truth has a way of conveying the Word of the Lord in such a way that the intent which was deeply seeded on the inside of you begins to surge out of your mouth. You'll come to yourself saying, "My God, I'm a sinner; I'm a man of unclean lips! My God, what has made me say that?" You said it because the Truth came and undressed a lie that was living within your temple!

PROPHETIC PRINCIPLE #7
Your father is identified through your actions.

We don't realize how blind we are until the Truth slaps us in the face. The force of Truth has a way of making us stagger. Often, when I am in my study pouring over the Scriptures investigating Greek and Hebrew words and finding new dimensions of the Word, I have to close the book and get up and walk awhile because the Truth has slapped me in the face! The study of God's Word is awesome in that you are constantly confronted with new realms of Truth!!

Division will provoke people to violence. Those that felt divided from Jesus would have taken Him but no man laid hands on Him. When God puts you on His assignment, no man can take your life. You have the power to lay it down and you have the power to take it up. No one determines your destiny except God. When you know who you are, no one can stop you. They'll make it harder for you, but opposition is the proof that you're on your right assignment! They'll initiate the struggle of intimidation, but a tree cannot come forth without struggling through the hard place. A baby cannot be born unless the process of contraction occurs.

Many of you are in situations that are overdue for productivity, and God is about to induce your labor! Some of you will start experiencing contractions in the Holy Ghost because there's a generation that must be saved! There's a generation that will not be able to wage war in the Christianity of our grandparents and of our parents. Many of you have embraced a form of godliness that has made you docile — many of you are turning the other cheek without gaining an understanding. The Bible says "Be meek," not weak!!

PROPHETIC PRINCIPLE #8
The true gospel brings liberation.

John 7:45-47:
> *Then came the officers to the chief priests and Pharisees; and they said unto them, Why have ye not brought him?*
> *The officers answered, Never man spake like this man.*
> *Then answered them the Pharisees, Are ye also deceived?*

There are certain religious leaders that will follow the pattern of Jesus' opposition. Pharisees and Sadducees will always find those of like spirit and attempt to silence the Truth. Satan's strategy to combat the Truth is to stir up the brethren against one another. Anytime you begin to represent the Truth, some folks are going to say you're deceived. But the witness of Truth is a reality! When Truth comes, something on the inside leaps within your spirit. It's almost like a game at an amusement park. Something on the inside lights up; a bell goes off and horns begin to blow within your innermost being when you've encountered Truth!

Verses 48-50
Have any of the rulers or of the Pharisees believed on him? But this people who knoweth not the law are cursed. Nicodemus saith unto them, (he that came to Jesus by night, being one of them,)

> ### PROPHETIC PRINCIPLE #9
> ## One can adapt to darkness.

Nicodemus was a ruler of the Jews. He was one that was in the upper echelon of society in the Nation of Israel. When he went to the Liberator, he didn't go openly. He found the obscurity of night, and visited Jesus privately to avoid recriminations.

Verses 51, 52
Doth our law judge any man, before it hear him, and know what he doeth?
They answered and said unto him, Art thou also of Galilee? Search, and look: .....

In other words, when you begin to identify with oppressed people, something will change in your language that will identify you with the oppressed. You'll start sounding like them. The concerns of the oppressed will become your daily concern, also. When you begin to embrace truth, others will begin to see that change has already manifested in you.

Verse 53
And every man went unto his own house.

Jesus states to the crowd that the devil is their father, which explained their murderous intentions and malicious falsehood. The devil is the father of lies and stands in the sharpest contrast to Jesus who speaks and is the Truth. The rejection of Truth is grounded in their origin, for they are, by nature, alienated from God.

PROPHETIC PRINCIPLE #10
Behavior is habitual. Change can feel like wrong.

And because I tell you the truth, ye believe me not. Which of you convinceth me of sin? And if I say the truth, why do ye not believe me?
He that is of God heareth God's words: ye therefore hear them not, because ye are not of God.

John 8:45-47

Why is it that some people cannot hear the words of Truth? Simply because they are not of God. It takes an anointing to sit under the truth. When the truth comes, it brings deliverance and blessing, yet can have an infuriating effect upon some people by stirring an anger that prompts them to throw stones. When the gospel is preached, people are going to be angry with you.

John 8:30,
As he spake these words, many believed on him.

Jesus preached to many individuals that were believers. He preached to individuals that had faith in God. Jesus was actually speaking in a systematic method; it was a set discourse. Jesus already understood His agenda and goals He was sent to accomplish.

You must continue to stay in a given place, in a particular state, relationship or expectancy. In other words, this is not a truth that you can look at for a moment and then walk back to your old ways, but it's a truth which you must embrace and into which you are compelled to walk. You cannot hear this truth and continue with the same false imagery on your walls. You cannot hear truth and not change your ways. You cannot hear truth and continue to eat the lie.

PROPHETIC PRINCIPLE #11
Don't be led by your feelings.

Verse 31
*Then said Jesus to those Jews which believed on him,
If ye continue in my word...*

"Word" means "the reasoning or the mental faculty of God". You have to continue in that which He has laid forth, the logos. And remaining in the area that is already laid forth systematically by our Lord and Savior, Jesus Christ. We must continue in His Word. God said, you'll be His disciples, you'll be His learners, His pupils.

Oppression produces black on black crime, for oppression will cause us to hate the image of God upon us. Oppression will cause our self-hatred to express itself in the defacement of property and in a penetrating lack of self-respect. Oppression will place a cry upon the lips of our women, for they will have a hard time finding males that are suitable providers. Oppression bears its own agony, for when one receives the gospel—the good news of Jesus Christ—one begins to recognize oppression and its devastating effects upon a people.

One cannot help but wonder - who are the real criminals? There's an ugly spirit that has blemished our minds. Someone has been manipulating our inheritance!

> **PROPHETIC PRINCIPLE #12**
>
> ## The gospel will evoke change.

As I perused the Encyclopedia Brittanica, one of the things I discovered is that our people have been further enslaved because they have been taught a European concept of Christianity. It was brought to us in a deliberate attempt to shackle our minds to our "massa's" and deaden our ability to think like God. Some would love to call what I am saying heresy, and will point at numerous black churches. They'll cite what happened to Allen, and recount how blacks left the Methodists and started their own division. They'll point at the black Baptists in Atlanta and recite how the blacks marched out of the white Baptist church and started their own. And I will gladly concur that blacks gathered together, but I must point out the unfortunate truth that we continued in the same theology that crippled us. The "massa's" concept of Christianity continued to echo through the lips of those who were conditioned towards their gospel. We were carriers of a theology that was not of God because had it been the truth, it would have made us free.

Bishop E. Bernard Jordan

CHAPTER THREE
In Living Color

While exploring the Encyclopedia, I came across some obscure information, which greatly disturbed my spirit. While reading about Pope Julius II and the Sistine Chapel ceiling, the Encyclopedia Brittanica reports: "The remainder of Michelangelo's career was largely controlled by his relationship with the papacy and from 1505 to 1516 the Vatican became the focal point of his artistic endeavors. Initially called to Rome to sculpt an enormous tomb for Pope Julius, II, Michelangelo completed only a fraction of the proposed sculptural program including the magnificent Moses and the fascinating new studies known as the 'Dying Slave' and the 'Rebellious Slave.'

A major reason for his inability to finish Julius' tomb was the immense project he undertook during 1508 to 1512 to execute on the ceiling of the Sistine Chapel a pictorial cycle devoted to the biblical history of humanity." During this period, the Church was beginning to emerge out of the crippling murkiness of the dark ages. Up to this time, the Madonnas and the Christ were normally depicted as black. Pope Julius gave Michelangelo a commission to start a project that has shaped the concept of Christ for centuries—- into the 1990's. His concept of a European Christ fills your walls and have enslaved your minds to a lie.

> **PROPHETIC PRINCIPLE #13**
>
> **Light can be painful.**

The encyclopedia continues to say, "The most sublime scene is the creation of Adam in which Michelangelo's new vision of human beauty first articulated in the David attained pictorial form. In the four years that he took to complete the ceiling, Michelangelo realized the full potential of the high renaissance style in the process, he changed the artistic vision of another great high renaissance master, Raphael, and altered the course of western art."

Michelangelo also painted the crucifixion of Peter and a portrait of Paul, yet the Bible says that Paul was mistaken for an Egyptian (Acts 21:38). You can't be mistaken for something you don't look like! Revelation gives us a vivid description of Jesus (Chapter 1) as bronze and His feet as if they were burned in a furnace. Images have been altered from the original description. Now, people will accuse me of trying to preach a black Jesus. Some will ask, "Are you trying to tell us that Jesus is black or are you just trying to get a Jesus that you can identify with as a people?"

No, I am bringing the truth of Who Jesus really was and Who He is! Now, you may ask the question, "Why a need to return to the original features of our Lord?" For several vital reasons!! Number 1, to restore the truth back into the lives of men. Next, to restore the self-esteem of the African race because our oppressor carried a Bible in one hand and a whip in the other. The image of Jesus presented to us echoed the image of our slave masters—-and they were the bearers of unspeakable cruelties and atrocities. Many have been able to accept the Lordship of Christ, yet are not free in their walk because they see Him as their oppressor. We are able to identify with the suffering of Jesus because His suffering was so similar to ours; hanging on wood, being stripped naked and whipped, being acquainted with grief, being a man of sorrows, being rejected of men, and being made subject to public ridicule and false accusation. Yet we never were able to change the image in our minds of the way He looked because of the picture we were beholding, therefore, a subtle fear of rejection clouds our perspective of He whom we call Lord and Master.

> **PROPHETIC PRINCIPLE #14**
>
> **Programs can be crippling. Don't depend on a system, but ask God for wisdom.**

The world must be restored to a consciousness of the physical reality of Christ and understand that God is a God of the oppressed people. If one were to accept the dictates of this society, one would begin to wonder if God is a racist. If you look at those that proclaim that they know Jesus, and compare the word of their lips with their actions towards African Americans, and other ethnic expressions, you would have to ask, "You are the seed of Abraham, and you say God is your Father and look at the way you are treating us! My God, you mean to tell me you are a partaker of His divine nature? If that is the nature of God, I don't want to accept it!"

What is the danger of this altered version of white Christianity? Number one, it promotes slavery. Number 2, it teaches Christians that if you're black and profess Christianity, you're supposed to be a good-slave and submit to whatever dictates emit from the mouths of white people...for they have knowledge of spiritual things...and you don't. You're not supposed to make any trouble. I hear it all the time! "Prophet Jordan, you need to cool it down a little bit." "Why don't you be nice?" "You're causing division in the Body." "You're offending people." "You're hurting people." "Why don't you preach a message on love?" "I think we need to call a prayer meeting and pray for the prophet....he sounds like he's bitter."

> **PROPHETIC PRINCIPLE #15**
>
> **A false godliness will make you docile.**

The voice of the oppressor will begin to say, "Calm down. Take it easy. Don't cause any disturbance. Blessed are the peacemakers for they are the children of God." The spirit of the oppressor is born of satanic influence, and will twist Scriptures to make them fit their manipulations.

We need to also understand that the incarnation of Jesus shows us what God had in mind concerning His plan of salvation. Now, when God came into this world we begin to notice some things. We see that God's plan of salvation spoke of His ministry to the poor. Somehow, God became incarnate with the poor. Jesus said, "Those that giveth to the poor, lendeth to the Lord." Jesus had a distinct ministry to the oppressed. To know Jesus is to know the divine side and the human side of Him. Many Americans want to worship the Christ but many don't want to look at Jesus the man. They want to look at the Christ so they can go around saying, "We're spirit." "There's no color in God." Well, that's a lie! How can you say there's no color in Him when the Scripture states His coloring? When the prophet Ezekiel looked up and said, "I saw as the color of amber..." (Ezekiel 1:27) John the revelator wrote, "His hair was like wool...." Revelation 1:14, "Any man that denies Jesus has come in the flesh is of the Antichrist." For any people to deny their cultural identity tells us two crucial truths; that they hate God, for it is He that determines your cultural identity, and that they hate themselves, for you cannot see that you are made in the image of Almighty God. When you hate yourself, you are incapable of loving others. You can only love thy neighbor as thyself.

PROPHETIC PRINCIPLE #16

"Be Meek," Not Weak!!"

It was the "white Christ-image" that held slaves in the bondage of slavery...never the black Jesus. The major barrier to converting the slaves was the slave holder who feared that the freedom Jesus offered the oppressed during his own time and the equality present throughout the New Testament might make the slaves think that they should be free and equal to the white population. This same barrier exists today in the minds of those white pastors who are afraid to allow blacks into governmental positions in the church.

Christianity was not given to blacks willingly until a plan had been formulated. That's why they didn't want blacks to be able to read because then they would become privy to truths that they did not want applied. Some of the slaves started reading, and began singing songs like "Go down Moses." They weren't following "servants be obedient to your masser." They stumbled over the stories of Moses and the Exodus and David going up against Goliath. A man by the name of Nat Turner was reading the Old Testament, and he read that God told the people to take the tools of their enemies. He stumbled on some truth, and he went from Preacher Nat Turner to General Nat Turner because he realized that this thing about "heaven in the by and by" is not making it! The Kingdom of God must manifest in the nasty "now and now!" Somehow he had a vision of the Kingdom of God coming to planet Earth! He was a prophet that encountered the truth of the Scriptures! Truth is dangerous when you get a hold of it!

PROPHETIC PRINCIPLE #17
The witness of Truth is a reality!

The proponents of black oppression perverted the truth to keep their lies alive. The "white Jesus" became their answer. They highlighted Scripture such as Genesis 9:25 to legitimize slavery and assuage their consciences. The used the Scripture to say that God supported human bondage. They convinced us that Ham was cursed, and people grew up thinking black people were ordained of God to be enslaved. Someone lied to you!! God never cursed Ham! As a matter of fact, the bible said Noah blessed his sons! God does not curse what He's already blessed!! The scripture says, "Cursed be Canaan."

We, as African Americans, are confronted by a generation that doesn't even want us to talk to them about our God because of the misrepresentation of the Kingdom of God. Salvation is connected to deliverance, which involves liberating activity. According to Webster's Dictionary, "deliver" means "to save, to rescue, to set free." It also means

> **PROPHETIC PRINCIPLE #10**
>
> ## The Devil is the father of lies.

"to assist at birth or to give birth to, to unburden oneself in discourse or to give up, abandon, resign, hand on to another, distribute like letters, parcel, ordered goods to addressee or purchaser or to launch or aim or to pronounce a blow, ball, or attack." We must understand that Christianity must be liberating activity and not enslaving acts! We can't sit in the salt shaker any longer!! We have to demonstrate the will of God in the earth, and stop talking about "one of these days in the great by and by!" We must break free of the shackles of passivity that have been placed upon our minds through the lies of our oppressors! We must get up off our "do nothings" and start businesses—obtain real estate. We need to stop looking for their programs to help get us over, but we need to know the God of our salvation and become empowered by Him! Get into the wisdom of God and talk to the Comforter who stands by your side and say, "Lord, show me what to do next!" Shake off the limitations and labels that this sinful society has told you to wear!! Understand that with God on your side, **NO THING IS IMPOSSIBLE UNTO YOU!!**

Bishop E. Bernard Jordan

CHAPTER FOUR
The Right Image and Right Message

Black slaves looked at Christ's actions, and not His skin color; although they saw Him as the white Christ. Just think what would have happened if they would have linked Christ's blackness and Christ's liberating power together!! I believe this is the next wave that is coming in the church of the Lord Jesus Christ: The Right Image and the Right Message!! There are people who are studying Greek and Hebrew, interpreting and equipped with an understanding of the Scripture. We're about to see the power of God be displayed in our generation!!

PROPHETIC PRINCIPLE #18

Truth brings deliverance and blessings.

In 1954, a black psychologist, Kenneth Clark, during his argument before the United States Supreme Court "Brown versus the Board of Education" case, stated how important it was for "black people, particularly black children to have positive black images." His research demonstrated that a bombardment of white images and symbols severely damaged black self-worth and self-esteem. Essentially, Clark's finding supported Malcolm X's observation that "black worship of white images, even Christ, is unhealthy and reflective of black people's psychological and emotional enslavement to a white racist culture." You've got to get the image of the lie out of your mind!

I am beginning to wonder if the reason they changed the image of Christ is because they understood the power of images, and that by exalting the European Christ, they would then obtain the power to become. Whatever you behold, you become. You will be changed into the same image, from glory to glory. Whatever you worship, you become. So, worshipping the "Christ-image" painted by Michelangelo will cause you to surrender your cultural identity and force you to become a parody; something other than what Christ has designed you to become. We need a true image of Jesus to be placed in our minds, for when our images change, our lives will change! Your walk will change! When your inner image changes, you will no longer walk around as a pauper but you'll begin to walk around as priests and kings unto God! When your image changes, your posture will change! When your image changes, your lifestyle will change!

We need to see the true image of Jesus. We need His image restored within us. Is this just to benefit blacks? No!! For if white people are able to see the humanity of Jesus, it would dethrone the superior attitude that pervades their cultures. They would stop being afraid of black men. They would stop being condescending towards our women.

Now, let me make this clear. I am not "racist" - I do not have the power to be racist. I don't have any military power, nor do I have any guns stashed away to enforce laws. So, according to Webster's dictionary, I don't have the power to be racist. However, I do have a love for my people, which is the responsibility of every individual - to love their people. After loving me first, and my own, then I love all.

> **PROPHETIC PRINCIPLE #19**
>
> **You cannot hear Truth and not change your ways.**

This message is designed to reach all of mankind, for the spirit of the oppressor is found in every ethnic strain. Blacks became our oppressors, for they assimilated "white thinking." "White well-being" became their primary goal in life.

America said, "Let us make a nigger." God said, "Let us make man." If you hear people pointing the finger at me with the accusation, "He is a racist," just say "No, he is guilty of reminding us who we are in the image of God."

Well, where does this put people that are non-black or that are not Latinos or not the oppressed? Well, it gives them an opportunity to repent of their oppressive actions. If they want to pick up the cross of

Jesus Christ in this hour, then they should be glad to pick up the struggle of black and/or oppressed people.

America will be forced to rethink her methods and priorities in the coming years. Capitalism cannot work unless it is oppressing a group of people. Yet the Spirit of God is not found among the oppressors, but in the camp of the oppressed. For they that are whole need not a physician, but they that are sick. Most cultures worship a god that looks like them. Now, you have to hear the spirit of what I'm about to reveal because it's like a bomb and you must understand what God has given you. The Asians put up their god, the Indians put up their gods, the Japanese have their religious system - every culture has their religion.

> **PROPHETIC PRINCIPLE #20**
>
> **Oppression will cause us to hate the image of God upon us.**

Somehow, God has put truth in the image of black people and He came in the form of blackness. No, we're not creating a black Jesus, we're restoring the original image of Jesus. We are dealing with history, and we got history from His story!

I heard someone say, "Now they have the African Heritage Bible and they've made all of the images black," as if they just changed them to black. No, they restored them back to the original image. The Bible tells us Jesus' feet were as bronze, and we know that if His feet were bronze, His facial color would not be different from His feet! The Bible also said, "His hair was as wool"— seems to me as if God had an Afro!

When we also understand that when God placed His seed in Mary, this also reveals to us the identity of God the Father. The writer of the Book of Hebrews declares that Jesus was the express image of the Father. God began with the original man in Africa. We must go on record saying that we know Africa was not the original name of the Continent. That was, again, a name that was given to us because it was all known as Ethiopia. The Bible says, "Ethiopia shall soon stretch her hands unto God" but we must understand that we have to read before that, it says, "princes shall come out of Egypt." In other words, leaders will come out from among our people and when leaders come forth out of the midst of our people, the nation will begin to stretch forth her hands unto God. Let me break it down to you another way; when Moses came forth, Israel could stretch forth her hand.

> **PROPHETIC PRINCIPLE #21**
>
> **The theology of the oppressor twists the gospel to suit their purpose.**

You're not looking for a system to change, you're trying to birth princes to come out of Egypt and when the deliverers come forth, you will stretch forth your hand. That's why there's a move of satanic conspiracy to destroy black leadership. That's why there's a move from out of the camp of the enemy to destroy any blacks that are progressing.

Usually, when the oppressor infiltrates those they are oppressing, it is not to learn and be taught how to be fathered, but they come to teach and give you their agenda to follow. They are out to cripple us. That's why we have many politicians that cannot bring deliverance to their community because they have taken the bribe. The oppressor fed them an agenda, and they trumpet what they've been bribed to trumpet, rather than speak the truth. We have black organizations that are ineffective because they are receiving white dollars. We believe that the wealth of the wicked is laid up for the righteous, but God wants us to be like father Abraham; where we will lift up our hands and say, "No man has made us rich but only Almighty God." When we submit to the principles of the Word of God, they will not control our agenda. God has knocked on the doors of many men and women with this word but the dollar took the message right out of their mouths.

> **PROPHETIC PRINCIPLE #22**
>
> **A European Christ fills your walls and has enslaved your minds to a lie.**

We have been so brainwashed to respond to the authority of white skin, that whenever one or two come into our midst, we feel a false sense of pride and get excited by saying, "Oh Wow! Guess what? We have whites with us now." We don't even let them sit long enough to begin to absorb our ways and be taught our agenda. The eagerness to feel accepted by them blinds our judgment. This is why, although we've gone around the corner in civil rights, we have ended back in the same neighborhood of racism. Hear the Word of the Lord!!

> John 8:30-31
> *As he spake these words, many believed on on him.*
> *Then said Jesus to those Jews which believed on him, If ye continue in my word, then are ye my disciples indeed.*

> **PROPHETIC PRINCIPLE #23**
>
> **When Moses came forth, Israel could stretch forth her hand.**

The only way you're going to become a disciple or a disciplined follower is by continuing in His Word. As a people, we need to understand the reason for the struggle. Struggle is not our enemy, but is the necessary catalyst to propel us to life. Maybe we've been out of the back of the bus too long. When we were denied the right to sit in the front, our vision for sitting in the front became a goal. Yet once that was attained, we didn't have a vision beyond the bus. We ride buses every day, but what bus companies do we own? We drive cars every day; what cars have we created? Now, some might say that black people have really advanced over the years, but what is advancement when all we've become are greater consumers? Where are our manufacturers? What are we building? What product have we created? Not a product that we are moving as part of someone else's strategy of success, but one which we've created? Where is the creativity that God put in us from the beginning? Where is the life that Father has given to you? What has this to do with the gospel? Well, if you don't have wealth, you cannot preach this message. You'll be bought off.

Bishop E. Bernard Jordan

CHAPTER FIVE
No Trains to Heaven

John 8:32-33
> *And ye shall know the truth, and the truth shall make you freee. They answered him, We be Abraham's seed, and were never in bondage to any man: how sayest thou, Ye shall be made free?*

How soon they forgot! They were in Egypt in the house of bondage. When the devil blinds you, he blinds you completely. The Israelites spent 400 years in slavery. Jesus was trying to get them to understand that they were in sin, which blinded them. They were not of God, for their father was the devil who is the father of lies.

Your consciousness must be awakened to the reality of the state that our people are in. Many of you are on a fast "train to heaven." You've been singing songs like "I'm going home on the morning train." You remember the song?

> "I'm going home on the morning train.
> The evening train may be too late.
> I'm going home on the morning train."

PROPHETIC PRINCIPLE #24

The Scripture indicates that Jesus was Black.

I hate to break this to you, but the ticket is cancelled! It's cancelled! The train is not running today! We have been so heavenly-minded until we're no earthly good! We have become like ostriches, burying our heads in the sand as genocide takes place! Young black men have become an endangered species. In New York City, as a people, we make up 33% of this city's population but 80% of the males that are in prison are black African-American and Latino-American males. Why is there an onslaught of arrests in minority communities when crime is just as rampant in the white communities? Why is it so important to them to get your sons in prison?

The spirit of the oppressor operating within American society has purposed again to make a nigger. They want to recreate the image of a slave, for the fraudulent vision of their superiority has not faded from their racist eyes. "Massa" tells our young men: "Just sign here, we'll give you a lighter sentence. Instead of going away for 10 years, we'll give you 3 months. Just say that you did it." "But I didn't do it." "Just say that you did." Listen...the oppressor never plays fair. They will use the ignorance that is in our community, and coerce our young men into signing confessions to crimes that they never committed. I have encountered so many young men who said they didn't commit the crime but signed the paper because they were told if they signed, they'll be put on probation. In their fear and intimidation, they agreed.

Our sons need to know not to compromise if they didn't commit the crime. There should be an understanding that truth is always the honorable way!! Stand in truth because truth will always prevail! Stand and say, "do what you must do, but I must tell the truth."

> **PROPHETIC PRINCIPLE #25**
>
> ## God is the God of the oppressed people.

There is a collective strategy to incarcerate our young men during their warrior years - between 13 and 30 - the years of their greatest strength. Many are slammed with long term prison sentences for acts of misdemeanor...while their white counterparts are slapped on the wrist, and sent home to the support of their culture that will assimilate their error and band together to forge their place in productive society. Our young men are faced with further rejection and dead end promises that crumble their hopes, dreams and desires. Prison robs a man of his manhood. When he goes in, he's given a number to replace his name. The system methodically strips his dignity. A person coming out of prison usually emerges extremely bitter because they have now experienced the injustice of a system that goes beyond punishment into the same level of criminality that they were supposed to rebuke. The ex-convict is labeled with a record which automatically locks them out of certain jobs. If he wants to get married and develop a family, it becomes extremely difficult for him to ever find gainful employment

> **PROPHETIC PRINCIPLE #26**
>
> **The Spirit of the oppressor is born of satanic influence.**

again, and he must suffer the indignity and shame of hearing his woman declare, "I'll take care of you." When she walked down the aisle, she thought she married a man but discovered he is now reduced to a child in her care.

She understands that by nature, women take care of children. His woman must then begin speaking and negotiating for him and pay the bills. After about a year or so, the frustration level rises to rage, and the marriage is destroyed. They're both fed up with his impotence, for you can't respect someone you're taking care of when they are supposed to be taking care of you. Eventually, the final blow to his manhood will come when she snaps her fingers and says, "I don't need you. You are a liability, I can raise these children by myself." That man, not knowing his identity or understanding the system that he's in, becomes a victim; his wife and children become victims; and the family is destroyed. The court system continues the cycle, and imprisons the man again for not supporting his children...and the indictment against his manhood continues. One wonders if the asylums for the insane have the wrong patients. And unfortunately, the Church is silent.

Now, a family has been produced out of a morass of confusion and chaos because the order of God is ejected from their lives. The system is programmed to destroy the mentality of our young boys. They become anti-social through the treatment they receive. Callous guards who turn their head at the organized crime within the walls of the prison, or abuse their authority, inflict fears and resentments that smolder until they turn into raging fires of hatred that refuse to be quenched by empty words. Our young men are made subject to sodomy to abolish their manhood and develop an appetite for that which is unnatural. Usually, rape is a common experience for any young boy that is thrown into prison. The emotional devastation experienced is so overwhelming that most young men are mentally crippled for the rest of their lives. The corruption of the penal system has reduced our jails to nothing more than legalized concentration camps.

Our government thinks nothing of paying $25,000 a year to put our sons in jail, but they won't make education freely accessible to motivate them to greatness. America must face a very bitter truth. Racism is a rampant bacteria that has infested the integrity of this nation.

> **PROPHETIC PRINCIPLE #27**
>
> ## Jesus had a distinct ministry to the oppressed.

Yet the Church of the Lord Jesus Christ must sound the Word of the Lord in this hour, for He is speaking a clear answer in the camp of the oppressed people.

> John 8:34, 35
> *Jesus answered them, Verily, verily, I say unto you, Whosoever committeth sin is the servant of sin. And the servant abideth not in the house for ever: but the Son abideth ever.*

I'm here to tell you, though you have been enslaved, you won't be a slave forever! You'll be a son forever — you'll be a son of God! For

NOW are we the sons of God!! (1 John 3:2) It does not yet appear what we shall be, but when He shall appear, we're going to be in His full Image, and in His full likeness!

> **PROPHETIC PRINCIPLE #28**
>
> **Many Americans want to worship the Christ, but many don't want to look at Jesus the man.**

The Bible tells us, He gave apostles, prophets, evangelists, pastors, and teachers for the perfecting of the saints, for the work of the ministry, for the edifying of the Body of Christ till we all come into the fullness of the stature of Christ (Ephesians 4:11-12) . For as many as received Him, to them gave He the power to become sons of God. (John 1:12)

We have to remove the hypnotic power of the false images that appear in media. We have to understand the enslavement of our minds to which we are constantly being subjected. Some of you think that concentration camps will never surface again, but don't stand on the shallow ground of vain imaginations! Some of us have become captive to the camps without walls; you're sniffing that white stuff up your nose, shooting your veins, destroying your brain cells, living in a stupor, and having the creativity of God siphoned out of you. Some of the oppressor's greatest experiments are taking place within the drug culture, and our ignorant and weak minded people respond to the thrill that is destined to kill.

> **PROPHETIC PRINCIPLE #29**
>
> # How can you say there's no color in Him when Scripture states His coloring?

Another camp without walls is illicit sex—our youth are bombarded with propaganda to experiment....are you big enough?....are you tight enough?...try this...try that...be safe...use condoms...take the pill...new devices...be sexy....teenage pregnancies and abortions abound without any sense of shame, and once again,....our ignorance is to blame! And you thought Hitler was dead! That spirit is manifest in America...it is time to fight the good fight of faith!

> John 37 says,
> *I know that ye are Abraham's seed; but ye seek to kill me because my word hath no place in you.*

There are those who say they're born-again, but they will seek to kill those who speak the word of liberation to a people. Everyone will not celebrate at the "coming out party!" There are some that look just like you who are not happy about the coming out. They'll fuss!! LOUDLY!! "Why must these issues be discussed by the church?" they'll whine. "What has this to do with the risen Christ? There's no color in God, and it doesn't make a difference. As long as I know that heaven is waiting for me, then that's all I need." They've been crippled. Their thoughts are limping along on a fraction of truth. Jesus' natural identity does make a difference! The Bible doesn't waste words. Every Word of God is infallible and has great significance. If Jesus' skin color didn't make a difference, I don't believe John, under the unction of the Holy Ghost, would have indicated the color of His feet. The Bible is the inspired Word of God, and no one has the authority to say that Jesus' color doesn't matter. Now whose word should we stand on, your's or God's?

PROPHETIC PRINCIPLE #30

When you hate yourself, you are incapable of loving others.

> *But now ye seek to kill me, a man that hath told you the truth, which I have heard of God: this did not Abraham.*
> *Ye do the deeds of your father. Then said they to him, We be not born of fornication; we have one Father, even God.*
> *Jesus said unto them, If God were your Father, ye would love me: for I proceeded forth and came from God; neither came I of myself, but he sent me.*
>
> John 8:40-42

To those Caucasian brethren who cannot digest what I am saying, please allow me to say this; If you were of the Father, if your Christianity and religion were of God, you wouldn't have tried to change our cultural identity. You would have never tried to make us "niggers" but you would have identified with us as men. You wouldn't call us "boy," even though we're 30+ years of age, and teach us to address your 12 year old son as "Mister Smith."

> Verse 42, ...
> *If God were your Father, ye would love me.*

Not hate me, and not burn crosses on my lawn. You would love me. You wouldn't come out with new laws saying, "Last hired, first fired." You would love me, and desire to compensate me for the losses we suffered as a result of the sins and failures of past generations. You would teach your children to love me, and not teach them ludicrous tales that I have a tail! You wouldn't teach them that I am an animal and my ancestors were monkeys. That is, if you loved me! ...For I proceeded forth and came from God; neither came I of myself ..." And for all the bleeding heart liberals that feel they've identified with "The Cause" of "civil rights;" equating homosexuality with racism...please allow me to say, ...I had no choice in this thing...but you do. You can choose to obey the laws of nature, and allow your organs to function in their proper use. If you're a man you're born with a penis and scrotum. You are born with the impulse and urge to insert your organ. Where you choose to insert it is a matter of choice. God created Adam and Eve...not Adam and "Steve!" Eve was equipped and "Steve" needs to be whipped! Eve had the hips and Steve had the lips! The sexual order of God is male and female. Even a dog knows not to mate with its own sex. Let's set the record straight!!!

I must inform you that America is not a Christian nation. You can't convince me that this is a Christian nation when homosexuality is increasingly embraced as "an alternative lifestyle." Our leaders are saying, "We need to give them rights, also. Let them teach your children." I don't want them teaching my children. A child is like a blank

> **PROPHETIC PRINCIPLE #31**
>
> **This cannot be a Christian nation when racism rules the seat of power.**

piece of paper. Anything that touches it leaves a mark. No, this is not a Christian nation, for it embraces the murder of the unborn when God says to be fruitful, multiply and replenish the earth. America cannot be a Christian nation when obscenity is trumpeted across the airwaves, and prayer is forbidden in schools. This cannot be a Christian nation when racism rules the seat of power. This cannot be a Christian nation when the Name of Jesus is profaned.

You may find other cultures that deviate from God's order and adopt homosexuality as part of their tradition, but there was a time that it was not found amongst Africans. Manhood was found in the mastery of the ways of nature, and since homosexuality is not found among the lower beasts, it was not duplicated until it was brought to the land by other cultures.

When we see our men and women embracing a homosexual lifestyle, then we are also seeing the infiltration of the ways of our oppressor.

CHAPTER SIX
Lies, Garbage and Trash

In John 8:43, Jesus said, "Why do ye not understand my speech? Even because ye cannot hear my word. Ye are of your father the devil, and the lusts of your father ye will do. He was a murderer ..." (God is describing your oppressor) "...from the beginning, and abode not in the truth, because there is no truth in him. When he speaketh a lie, he speaketh of his own: for he is a liar, and the father of it."

Our lives have been saturated with lies, garbage and trash. Hollywood sold us images that became fixed in our minds. Who will ever forget Charlton Heston as Moses in "The Ten Commandments?" The drama was wonderful, but it's not Bible. Moses grew up in Egypt and was black he was readily accepted as Pharaoh's son....he looked like him! His wife was Ethiopian...a different nation, but she was black!

The tribes of Israel were black. Ephraim and Manasseh were two tribes that had African or a Hematic mother Genesis 41:45-52. They all looked the same in that region! The Angel of the Lord spoke to Joseph and told him to take Mary and the baby Jesus into Egypt to hide. If they looked like the images that we're bombarded with today, they would have stood out like sore thumbs!

> **PROPHETIC PRINCIPLE #32**
>
> ## You can only love thy neighbor as thyself.

There will be those that will say, "I have a problem with Bishop Jordan's message." Just ask them who their father is!

There will be scholars that will go through the Bible seeking to find the whites in Scripture. Delilah was a Philistine, and that's of Hematic descent. Shem and Ham looked alike. They intermarried with each other.

> *And as Paul was to be led into the castle, he said unto the chief captain, May I speak unto thee? Who said, Canst thou speak Greek? Art not thou that Egyptian, which before these days madest an uproar, ...*
>
> Acts 21:37-38

Now, there's no doubt about what color Paul was. He was an educated Egyptian, a black man.

Acts 13:1 says, "Now there were in the church that was at Antioch certain prophets and teachers;..." Not ushers. There are many blacks

> **PROPHETIC PRINCIPLE #33**
>
> **Christianity was not given to Blacks willingly until a plan had been formulated.**

who belong to white churches whose pastors stick them in the parking lot to usher. Leadership development is never pursued. You can sing and dance, but you can't make decisions. Listen, I know I'm going to anger some people, but the crude fact is that blacks have no business sitting under white leadership in the church in this particular age. Why? Because they do not think much of you. The slave mentality still exists, and the only thing you can ever be to them is stock. This is the common dialogue:

White Pastor: "Pay your tithes."
Black Member: "I feel as though God called me into ministry."
White Pastor: "Go usher."
Black Member: "I feel as though God has given me a pulpit ministry."
White Pastor: "Well, you can sing. Ya'll can sing good. Join our choir. We'll even let you lead."

When the song is over, you will have to sit down because they won't allow you to bring inspired revelation in the pulpit. Yet, you'll sit in those churches docile, giving your tithe faithfully, never bothering the pastor. In fact, you don't even know where he lives nor do you know his phone number. He's not walking in your neighborhood past 12:00 midnight. He won't bury your baby, and he hasn't grown up in your community. He does not have a word to speak to you because he cannot identify with your problem. He knows nothing of your struggle. He'll be the first to ask, "What has color got to do with it as long as we just love Jesus?" He won't talk to you about your sons that are being imprisoned. He won't educate you about your genocide. He's not going to talk to you about the devastation areas that is taking place in your community. He says you can shout and say everything's going to be all right.

PROPHETIC PRINCIPLE #34
God never cursed Ham.

In the Scripture, we see blacks in leadership in the early church.

> *Now there were in the church that was at Antioch certain prophets and teachers; as Barnabas, and Simeon that was called Niger, and Lucius of Cyrene, and Manaen, which had been brought up with Herod the tetrarch, and Saul.*
>
> Acts 13:1

Simeon and Lucius were black men; Niger and Cyrene were located in Africa. Simeon, Lucius and Manaen were three black men who functioned in the leadership of the church at Antioch.

Now, in Acts 8, Philip was in a revival. Verses 26 and 27 states, "And the angel of the Lord spake unto Philip, saying, Arise, and go toward the south unto the way that goeth down from Jerusalem unto Gaza, which is desert. And he arose and went: and, behold, a man of

Ethiopia, an eunuch of great authority ..." (He wasn't a slave. He had

> **PROPHETIC PRINCIPLE #35**
>
> **Christianity must be liberating activity and not enslaving acts!**

authority. He wasn't a caricature out of a Tarzan movie, swinging on ropes and climbing trees, as so many have been led to believe about men from Ethiopia) "... under Candace queen of the Ethiopians, who had the charge of all her treasure, and had come to Jerusalem for to worship." Notice, here is an Ethiopian black Jew going to Jerusalem to worship.

Verse 28,
> *"Was returning, and sitting in his chariot read Esaias the prophet."*

This was a notable sight; a black man who was a reader! The Ethiopian eunuch was reading the Scriptures. Let me tell you something, Europe did not bring the gospel to us, we brought the gospel to them! The story is frequently told of sympathetic white Christians that introduced Christianity to some poor ignorant heathen slaves in 1619. This lie is undressed, for the Bible tells us we were there from the beginning! Someone stole your history and lied to you, and you believed it!

Verses 29-32,
> *"Then the Spirit said unto Philip, Go near, and join thyself to this chariot. And Philip ran thither to him, and heard him read the prophet Esaias, and said, Understandest thou what thou readest? And he said, How can I, except some man should guide me? And he desired Philip that he would come*

> *up and sit with him. The place of the scripture which he read was this, He was led as a sheep to the slaughter; and like a lamb dumb before his shearer, so opened he not his mouth:."*

Contrary to common belief, we don't have to accept the stigma that has haunted us for so long. We are not "Johnny-come-lately" in the

> **PROPHETIC PRINCIPLE #36**
>
> **We must get up off our "do nothings" and start businesses...obtain real estate.**

things of God! When some of our own misguided people state Christianity is a white man's religion, you can divulge the truth to them intelligently. You must let them know they're mistaken and show them the lie.

Church history records that Rome didn't start embracing the gospel until the reign of Constantine. Formerly, idolatry was the form of worship. The influence of idolatry eventually corrupted Christianity, and brought about an influx of error. When you start in error, you continue in error.

Christianity is meant to become liberating activity and not justification for acts of enslavement. Black slaves looked at Christ's action, not the skin color though they saw Him as a white Christ. We were able to identify with the suffering Christ, yet could not see ourselves triumphant. Most of us live our entire lives hanging on the cross, because we have no image of victory in our minds. We were taught to identify with Christ—and rightly so—but the only image that many of us saw was the suffering Christ. The next wave of the Spirit of God is going to be a wave that's going to unveil the Jesus in His Personhood, inclusive of His black skin, fighting for the liberation of black people in a society that has systematically strategized their destruction.

PROPHETIC PRINCIPLE #37
Shake off the limitations.

We must uproot the enemy in society. We must get our people out of the projects. America is always seeking for "projects;" science "projects," art "projects"...!" Don't you realize that black people were stuck in projects to live on top of each other so they can be studied? But don't you realize that you were never created to become someone's experiment? "Let's see how they act. When we take the father out of the home, the mother becomes strong and start having problems with the children. Good. What else? Now, the mother has to go out and get the food. The family unit is crippled, now what will they do? Good...the children are stealing and doing drugs. What will they do next?" They performed experiments with rats and monkeys, and after outgrowing that level, longed for a human specimen. And they see you as the closest thing!

Using economic feasibility as an enticement, projects became "the way out." Close confinement became their "project" while many of us thought we found the best way to make ends meet. Marriages faltered and adultery ran rampant. The children started running with gangs and found "fathers" in their peers. The aberrant lifestyle of living on top of each other stumped our creativity and stole our dreams. Our vision became limited. We would step out of our door and practically into someone else's apartment. Privacy disappeared through paper walls that transmitted secrets that should not have been told. Bedrooms and bathrooms lost their intimacy...and the vortex of rage increased as self hatred grew in the violation of natural habitat. For we are a people who were created for land, vast expanses of land that are long and wide. That's why our songs echo the longing of generations past for the haunting memories of Canaan land.

> **PROPHETIC PRINCIPLE #38**
>
> **Truth is not a philosophy but Truth is a Person.**

We have to get back in touch with the land. Kingdom mentality encompasses real estate. The nature of God is to possess land...you are commanded to take dominion and possess the land. When we begin to understand this, we're going to stop being America's pet project and move out of the laboratories!! This is not an easy lesson to learn. They experimented on me, too. In the early 1960's when they started busing us poor, underprivileged black kids into their schools, I was in the second grade. I was forced to see a counselor every week, where I was given crayons to draw pictures of my home so they could study my psyche. Some of you don't even realize when you go to the hospital that you become a project. During the 1950's, black men were infected with syphilis - they became a project—-an experiment. You have to pray over your food before you eat it. You may be part of a project! You'd better get over into the Holy Ghost!! You'll understand this thing better in the by and by, but if I were you, I would get an education in the nasty now and now!

What does this have to do with Christianity? God's Spirit is moving among enslaved people and He's raising up deliverers! Men are going to become the prophets, priests and kings of their households! Folks will start educating their children, and become individuals that will say, "I will not compromise. I'm about to take a new stand for God." God's calling for change. I don't know about you, but I've been in prayer, and I keep hearing God saying, "Reformation." I don't know how He's going to bring it about, but I know He brought Israel out without an army as men know. When you have God on your side, it's more than the whole world against you.

> **PROPHETIC PRINCIPLE #39**
>
> **Whatever you behold, you become. Whatever you worship you become.**

As we deal in the area of undressing the lie, we begin to see, according to John's gospel, Jesus tells us that we shall know the truth and the truth shall make us free. But we are also discovering that there are many people that do not want the truth to be heard, neither do they want the truth to be known. As we search throughout the Scriptures concerning our heritage as Christians and as believers, we have a responsibility in society to proclaim truth and to proclaim righteousness. We must understand, especially those of us who have been victimized, that we must protect ourselves from being victimized and also become a voice to victims.

When we look at the word, "undress," we understand that it means "to take off the clothes". A lie means "to speak softly, intentionally or intentional false statement, to deceive an individual or to give a false

> **PROPHETIC PRINCIPLE #40**
>
> **We need a true image of Jesus to be placed in our minds.**

impression." Jesus spoke to this particular group of individuals and encouraged them to remain in His Word. The Bible says that when we remain in His Word, we are His disciples indeed.

Truth is not a philosophy but Truth is a Person. We previously mentioned how Michelangelo changed the features of Jesus so that we ended up with a different image of Christ on our wall, and they have tucked away the original Image, and the original Complexion. You still may wonder why this is important. Actually, you should be wondering about the liars because if they lied in one area, how many other areas have they lied in? If you are of God, you will love the truth.

Now, how Jesus looked bears repeating for those who say, "It's unimportant;" for these are the people who need to take up a dialogue with the Holy Ghost who gave the description:

> *And in the midst of the seven candlesticks one like unto the Son of man, clothed with a garment down to the foot, and girt about the paps with a golden girdle. His head and his hairs were white like wool, as white as snow, and his eyes were as a flame of fire. And his feet like unto fine brass, as if they burned in a furnace;...*
>
> Revelation 1:13-15

The picture that I'm seeing in God's Word is not the picture that I'm seeing on most living room walls. The verse, "..and His feet like unto fine brass, as if they burned in a furnace:" places a demand on artists to cease from drawing a lie and to begin to draw the truth. It places a responsibility on preachers to preach the truth and to take the lie out of their sanctuary. "It doesn't make any difference, Preacher." Well, drawing something other than what is in the Scripture is presenting a false image.

> **PROPHETIC PRINCIPLE #41**
>
> **The oppressor distorts the Gospel by distorting the image of Jesus. Jesus is the Liberator.**

Let me point out something here - there weren't any chemicals then as we have today that could polish brass to make it lighter. So, get a vision of brass before it's polished, along with the fact that the writer of the Book of Revelation, under the inspiration of the Holy Ghost, made sure that he put an emphasis there so you wouldn't change it. As you know, there's yellow and white gold and knowing the minds of men, he emphasized, "...as if they burned." My mother used to tell me, "Watch what you're heating up or you'll burn it." I have yet to see something burnt that does not come out black.

I know some of you aren't ready for this and are still wrestling with it. Some are still having a problem, but we are in the Word of God. This isn't something I made up. I haven't stated I had a vision of Jesus, and I'm not trying to get you to believe my vision. I'm simply teaching you the Word of God. Some will even say, "I have a problem with looking at one Scripture, Preacher." Well, let's go to Daniel 7, but first let me point out the amusement of racist people who can't handle one Scripture when it comes to proving something about us, but they are the ones that took one Scripture and misinterpreted Ham and enslaved an entire nation. They didn't have two or three; they took one verse and hung an entire theology that God had cursed black people. But to prove that Jesus is black, there must be more than one Scripture. Pardon my sarcasm; it's all right, for God is on the side of the victim!

Daniel 7:9:
> *I beheld till the thrones were cast down, and the Ancient of days did sit, whose garment was white as snow, and the hair of his head like the pure wool: his throne was like the fiery flame, and his wheels as burning fire.*

I'm not through with Scripture yet; while you're picturing Jesus' Afro, turn to Daniel 10:6

> *His body also was like the beryl, and his face as the appearance of lightning, and his eyes as lamps of fire, and his arms and his feet like in colour to polished brass ...*

PROPHETIC PRINCIPLE #42

The oppressor cannot deliver the people they've oppressed.

Many of you are going through the Concordance right this minute, going to the book of your oppressors hoping He'll amplify the lie of your traditions. I have news for you....He's not going to amplify your lies, no matter how familiar or nice they feel to your heart. That's why we have to have our own scholars and our own writers, for they must be charged to open up our understanding of Scriptures that we have read over and over through the gospel of racism.

There are many people that will see this truth plainly. We don't even have to go to the Word to prove it. We can go to the archaeologists of the day and let them begin to search the facts, but there will be many that still will not embrace the truth. It's time to tell the truth.

Bishop E. Bernard Jordan

CHAPTER SEVEN
The Liberating Power of the Gospel

We must now link Christ's blackness and Christ's liberating power together for this is the next wave and the next move of the Spirit of God. It's a spirit of truth that's going to begin to prevail throughout the Body of Christ. When this message comes, we will lose many on the way; whites as well as blacks. God wants this message to be preached so He can kill the idol of racism that is existing within your very heart....within your very soul. Your very consciousness is being pricked and exposed through the power of the Truth.

It's very difficult to challenge individuals that have grown up in a system that has been trained and taught that anything other than white is inferior. Now, this is not only for African-Americans, it is also concerning Latinos. They have another battle with liberation with which they must wrestle.

> **PROPHETIC PRINCIPLE #43**
>
> **The spirit of the oppressor is found in every ethnic strain.**

Christianity, as we know it today, has not been liberating to our children. The only black person that they want to amplify in the Bible is Ham. You must know what you are wrestling with and what we are up against. We are dealing with a system of theology that has been perpetuating error and deliberately proclaiming it as the truth.

Kenneth Clark's research also supports Malcolm X's observation that black worship of white images, even Christ, is unhealthy and reflective of black people's psychological and emotional enslavement to a white racist culture.

In July 31, 1966, black clergy leaders issued a statement in the edition of the New York Times that endorsed "black power." It took the black church to come through Civil Rights to find out that integration looked like it wasn't going to work and began to have to endorse "black power." Now, let's understand what "black power" means. Most of the time when we hear the words "black power," we immediately grasp negative images of riots and blood running in the streets. But let's look at it this way; see God's power in black people because all power is ordained and it comes from God. Now this statement opened by describing the contemporary American theme as one where conscienceless power meets powerless conscience. See, you have a conscience but you don't have any power. You're dealing with folks that have power but no conscience. It says that whites who have wealth and no moral conscience are dealing with blacks that have moral conscience and no power. This condition now puts the white male in a position to usurp authority and act as a god in the destiny of a people by determining where they would live, their economic destiny, etc.

> **PROPHETIC PRINCIPLE #44**
>
> **America said, "Let us make a nigger." God said, "Let us make man."**

The black church began to wake up and began to address the root of the problem. The message of liberation is the revelation of God as revealed in the incarnation of Jesus Christ. Freedom is the gospel. Jesus is the Liberator, thus the black patriots and we, ourselves, know this reality despite all attempts of the white church to obscure it and utilize Christianity as a means of enslaving blacks. When there's an uprising, they trigger the docile Christians to say, "Now you need to be good Christians, and don't make waves. Calm down. Just pray, God's going to change it one day."

The demand that Christ, the Liberator, imposes on all men requires all blacks to affirm their full dignity as persons and all whites to surrender their presumption of superiority and abuses of power.

We are not creating black images in the Bible. He is Who He is. We're just proclaiming the truth because too many people are being harmed by a lie. You've bought into the lie when you say, "It doesn't make any difference what color God is." It made some difference to

Pope Julius, II, that's why he had Michelangelo paint a white Jesus in the ceiling of the church and that image today is in the minds of people all over the world...the image of a Christ that never existed.

> **PROPHETIC PRINCIPLE #45**
>
> **Most cultures worship a god that looks like them.**

Sad to say, but as many people's eyes become open, that Jesus Christ was black, they will walk out of Christianity rather than bow to a person of color. In their understanding, they're saying, "Never!" Someone brought a February 1994 issue of Ebony magazine to me, which contained an article by Lisa C. Jones, talking about blacks in the Bible. I just want you to see another aspect so you can begin to understand there is a balance to this. The article opens: "Although films, books and art depict most biblical characters as blond and blue-eyed Europeans, a growing body of research indicates that blacks or people who would be considered as blacks today, were among the major actors in the Bible which is generally called the greatest Book of all time. 'Over the years, African-Americans have been introduced to a form of Christianity that was largely recast through the European culture' says, Dr. Cain Hope Felder. A New Testament language and literature Professor of Howard University School of Divinity, an author of several books on the subject says, 'We are not creating something new, we are going back and recovering what was always there.' The Queen of Sheba, Zipporah, Moses' Cushite wife, Deborah the Judge, Prophet Jeremiah's right-hand man, Ebed-Melech and Sarah's Egyptian handmaiden, Hagar, are among the many royal black personalities mentioned in the Bible.

> ## PROPHETIC PRINCIPLE #46
>
> **There's a move of satanic conspiracy to betray black leadership.**

Although the presence of blacks in the Bible dates back to the 18th Century, it is only in the past 25 years that black scholars and ministers have made major breakthroughs on a subject that has been practically ignored or suppressed by white religious authorities." He also stated, "In any case, black preachers, scholars and historians are determined to establish the presence of black kings, queens, war leaders and women of the Bible as part of the missing link in black history. 'The question isn't where are the blacks in the Bible, Dr. Selder said during a telephone interview, but where are the whites?'" It awakens some questions.

Many that have said the Bible is a white man's book. This is so far from truth because God started with people of color.

Capitalism can only work if it's oppressing someone. It thrives on the exploitation of the weaker. God chose to tabernacle among those that are going to exploited and among those that will be made victims. God entered into the world poor; He was born of a poor family. He's a symbol of an individual coming into the earth overcoming the odds. You've been ordained to overcome the odds. When He came, He was despised and rejected of men. When you are called of God, you will be despised, and rejected of men. God usually raises up individuals that are rejects. He elects rejects. He chooses those society says, "Won't make it, can't make it, and whom they say have not been destined to make it." God also came into society oppressed. He was born of a nation that was oppressed.

There is a cost for preaching this message. We get all kinds of strange phone calls; people saying, "What he's preaching is unnecessary." Well, the fact that it disturbs them shows it's necessity. "I don't want to hear you any more until you change your message." Those kinds of remarks are exactly why we have to keep preaching it. If it has angered you, then maybe we're getting somewhere. There just might be hope because anger is the first thing that needs to be produced before change can come.

> **PROPHETIC PRINCIPLE #47**
>
> **When the oppressor infiltrates those they are oppressing, it is not to learn and be taught.**

Now, there are those that say this message is only for blacks. That is very far from the truth. If it was only a message for black people, then why would your racist heart be disturbed? If it wasn't for you, it wouldn't affect you. We must also speak to blacks that are disturbed. If they become uncomfortable and start saying, "What are the whites thinking about this? Maybe he should preach something else," for who you are concerned about tells us who you really love.

No one in the educational system, when told they were going to learn about Columbus discovering America, asked, "What do you think blacks are going to say about it?" "We'll start their history from slavery and keep reminding them, and give them a whole month, the shortest month in the year, and we'll make sure we teach black history...and constantly remind them that they were slaves. We won't mention the fact that they're descendants of kings and queens but descendants of slaves." No one was concerned with whether you were offended or not. When they put messages on television linking you with monkeys and apes, how many asked, "What do you think blacks will think about it?" They were not interested in your feelings of shame, embarrassment or anger. When they used National Geographic magazine's pictures of remote African tribes whose concept of beauty was the antithesis of western ideology, who worried about the ridicule that you would be subjected to?

Isn't it interesting that the black cake is called "devil's food cake" and the white cake, "angel food cake?" Who asked, "What do you think blacks will think?" No one was concerned. We're dealing with a demonic mindset. Christianity must begin to erase certain teachings that have come out of western civilization, such as, black is connected with evil. This is a message for all people. It will liberate all men, if they embrace the gospel. Let me prepare you - the cost for preaching this message is high. To call Jesus black is to say to European theologians, "You're wrong." Understand the latent power struggle. See, a person that names something controls it. To call Jesus black is to let Europeans know that we will not submit to your white Christ. To call Jesus black is to call for the oppressor to bring a proper understanding to their community concerning the incarnation. What is frightening are those people who say it doesn't make any difference what color He is.

PROPHETIC PRINCIPLE #48

Eagerness for acceptance will blind your judgment.

The Bible states, "Any man that says Jesus did not come in the flesh is of the anti-Christ." People can spiritualize this all they want—-but they are in error. God wants you to focus on His incarnation. He wants you to identify with the form He came in.

> **PROPHETIC PRINCIPLE #49**
>
> **Struggle is not our enemy, but is the necessary catalyst to propel us to life.**

To call Jesus black is to call America to a national repentance, for she must embrace the righteousness of God and put away the lie of the white Christ. Why not portray the image of the Christ the way it is supposed to be? Jesus was a black man sent to deliver a black people in a world governed by Europeans who were oppressing people of color in their day. Jesus picked His disciple, Peter, who was a Zealot. The Zealots were a revolutionary group that had spurred a number of rebellions against Rome.

If Jesus walked the earth in the 1960's stating He would make fishers of men, He would have looked for radical individuals; drug dealers - "Come follow Me!" - "Let's go down to the Black Panther Party - "Come follow Me." He wouldn't have chosen "nice, religious" folks, for they would be the Pharisees and Sadducees. Their religiosity and sense of superiority would have disqualified them. Jesus chose radical people. He would have stopped by the way of the prisons looking for those who were coming out - "Come follow Me." People have a romanticized view as to who the disciples were, which is the image of a lie that must be dethroned.

Bishop E. Bernard Jordan

> **PROPHETIC PRINCIPLE #50**
>
> # When the devil blinds you, he blinds you completely.

Jesus came to rebuild His nation out of oppressed people. Israel was an oppressed nation. America is oppressed, and needs to be rebuilt upon a foundation of the truth. However, before we can rebuild our nation, we must first rebuild ourselves.

In reality, all black people came from Africa because the first man, Adam and Eve came from the Continent that was called Africa. We are the fathers of civilization, the fathers of science and conceptualization and the patriarchs of the human race. You are not inferior....far from it! Rediscover who you are! The European world teaches that they are the people who are the fathers of healing so when they tell you that Hippocrates is the father of medicine, you must understand that Imhotep, preceded him by over a thousand years in Egypt. American doctors are taking the wrong oath! The father of the original concept of human healing was a short black man. He laid the foundation for, not only medicine, but pyramid construction, military strategy, philosophy, and poetry....all at the same time.

God has given you a great mind! He has enabled you to THINK! Despite what your teachers and your coach may have told you, you were not created to play ball as the boundary of your existence! You were created for more than their entertainment! Your mind is able to calculate science and math! Don't let them tell you that you don't qualify because "you don't have the mind for it". The system is evil, and will deliberately attempt to destroy your self-image.

PROPHETIC PRINCIPLE #51

Don't compromise your innocence

Television is corrupt. Boycott it! The images are programmed to enslave our children's minds; hypnotizing them into a perennial lethargy that programs them for failure. We look at what takes place in media and see what our children are beholding; such as the show they called, "Good Times" where the man can't find a job. One of the women doesn't know where her man is and has a child without a father - Good Times. The oldest son, who is supposed to be the one that should carry the mantle of his father and be the one that fills in the gap in case the father leaves the throne, is acting like a fool - and they call it Good Times. Black folks living in the projects - and they call it Good Times. We have to get our people out of the projects!

The lie concerning all of these images brings enslavement to the black man who was already experiencing death and devastation. The Europeans had to prove once and for all the superiority of the European mind over its African fathers. It was the revolt of the son against the father. In other words, Socrates stole many of his concepts from African philosophers. Present day scientists are still trying to figure out how to build pyramids so they can steal that, too.

A hundred years from now, if civilization is still going on, and things don't change, some of your great-great-grandchildren will be saying, "Blues and jazz were created by the Europeans" and a name of some white individual will be exalted, saying he was the father of jazz, blues, gospel, and soul music. Error is perpetuated because we neglect the documentation of our historical records. We must become writers, documenting our achievements and putting them in safe deposits boxes. Hold them and pass them down to your sons. Don't think your history can't be robbed again! The very thing that God put in you to create and invent will become a lie proceeding out of the mouth of your oppressor. It's time to tell the truth! If we do not build and retain the image of God within us as a people, then we will embrace the animalistic image that has been fed to us. If we continue to view the lie, we will become the lie.

> **PROPHETIC PRINCIPLE #52**
>
> **Truth is always the honorable way!**

Christianity should re-program and renew your mind. It should instill dignity and self-worth. When you become born again, your head should be lifted up, not hung down.

The accelerated form of the rites of passage should be embraced. Our men must exodus from boyhood into manhood. We must begin to identify ourselves independently of our oppressor.

We must dispense with the unreasonable longing to be "just like them." Cease crying for integration. We want to be with them so bad! Why? Because we've been brainwashed to think they're superior, and we're inferior. They have a "more superior" education, so we want what they have. They have "more superior" neighborhoods, so we wanted to live with them. And now you've got everything they have.....and where are you today? You see what happens when you pray things that's contrary to the will of God? There are some things that are not God's will for you to obtain, but He'll give it to you just because you cried and lusted for it. You thought what you had was inferior; but you didn't know that God had put greatness on the inside of you. God gave you the ability to go into the field and pick up roots, "to take care of the fever." You didn't even know what it was but it healed you! Our mothers went into the woods, pulled up something, gave it to us to drink and it caused that stomach ache to go away! Some brainwashed folks told you it was witchcraft and said you were "working roots."

> **PROPHETIC PRINCIPLE #53**
>
> **Prison robs a man of his manhood.**

Your white doctors called it "stupid medicine," but God had put a science on the inside of you which you didn't go to school to learn. It came to you by nature. Nobody teaches the spider how to spin his web, either....it's in him by nature. Today, it is amazing to discover that the very thing that was stripped form you has now become a very elite form of medicine with prestigious titles like "herbology," "homeopathic medicine," and "naturopathy." And because we despised the voice of our elders, we must invest thousands to learn the surface of an art which was ours by divine impartation. Your mother didn't have to pay a dime because she just knew what root to pull up, and she knew how to move the poison aside and let you know you can't take that. She knew how to put certain types of leaves on a broken leg and tie it up; she didn't have casts and crutches. Your ancestors knew what to pull out of the field because they knew that the leaves were placed there by God for the healing of the nation. You ran from the very tools that God gave you!

PROPHETIC PRINCIPLE #54

Racism has infested the integrity of this nation.

No other people on the earth moan like we moan! When we couldn't find words to express their songs, we had a language of the spirit that brought melody to the groans of suffering.

And there were those of us that grew up in the Church despising the voice of our elders. We "integrated" into the white churches, and when we attempted to move in our cultural expression of worship and prayer, we were told "Stop! That's demonic and soulish! It doesn't take all of that!" We left our cultural worship and lost our identity. We removed ourselves from the very things that God put in us designed to bring deliverance to us as a people.

The black preacher became the prophet, for he merged with the soul of the people and spoke on behalf of the people to God, and at the same time, he became the voice of God to the people. There was something in their delivery that enabled them to sway the nation. Men like Malcolm X and Martin Luther King spoke under an anointing for oratory. They had a way with words, which was something that you could not learn at Harvard or Morehouse. Homiletics could not instill their passion. There was an indefinable edge to their speech that was birthed in the midst of their struggle that bore the mark of the Divine.

There was something in your music that could interpret the unspoken, and the song caused your spirit to soar in places your spirit could not go. There's a power of deliverance in your music. There's some-

> **PROPHETIC PRINCIPLE #55**
>
> **Some of the oppressor's greatest experiments are taking place within the drug culture.**

thing about music that makes you sway. You can't stand still, and you have great difficulty responding to Orthodox worship - that's not you! You can't stand there with your hands half-mast and recite the catechism! There's something in you that causes your body to sway when the music plays; something about you when you get down in prayer that makes you rock. Amen! You didn't know anything about the seven Hebrew words for praise, but you always moved in them! You didn't know the theology of faith, but you knew what faith was! There were times in the service when the Spirit of God began to move, and you'd begin to shabach and rock from side to side! Something would move on the inside of you which caused you to speak in tongues! God is trying to reconnect you to what He's put on the inside of you! You're trying to get the Hammond B-6 organ out of your worship and there are white churches trying to get the Hammond B-6 in! You're trying to stop your dancing, and they're trying to get into dancing! Don't deny your heritage...it's full of riches untold!!! Tap the power God has instilled within your inner most being!!

When you begin to understand liberation, you'll understand that it demands growth. God is bringing us into a place where we're beginning to understand ourselves. We must progress from self-knowledge to mastery. When you get into a knowledge of yourself and who He made you to be, you're going to move into mastery. You are not an inferior being. You're not low on the totem pole. Understand that Jesus places His Spirit in the camp of the oppressed, the destitute, the

PROPHETIC PRINCIPLE #56

The Bible doesn't waste words.

naked, and the abused. He comes as a God of the oppressed. When God brings us into worship, Jesus is in our midst. Where the Spirit of the Lord is, there's liberty. When we begin to hear this gospel in the light of the Word of God, the Spirit of the Lord will bring liberation in the mind, and in our thinking. He'll take a boy and make him a man. He'll take a frustrated woman and make her a lady. He'll help a single parent and fill the lack, fill the void. A man who has run away from supporting his children will find His seed, when the Spirit of the Lord comes. Some of you are fighting for your seed, for loved ones, and for family members; but if you embrace the gospel of the Kingdom, you'll find Liberty standing at your door! This message will do something radical on the inside of the lives of people. Some people will be astounded and some will be shaken up, but if you embrace it in the spirit that it is given, it will liberate you. Some people will walk and act differently, and some will lose "friends" along the way because when you start to undress the lie and tell the truth, everyone isn't going to celebrate your victory. There are those that will despise your coming to the knowledge of the truth, for they have the most to lose from your enlightenment.

I must say that I'm glad to be a victim, for I know God is on my side! He's on the side of the oppressed; on the side of those that are cast down. You shall know the truth and the truth will make you free!

> *Then Jesus said to those Jews that believed Him, If*
> *ye continue in my word, then are ye my disciples indeed.*
> John 8:31

Once you come into sonship and understand that you are a son of God, a partaker of His divine nature, you are made free and cannot be bound again if you continue in His Word.

> *I speak that which I have seen with my Father: and ye do that which ye have seen with your father. They answered and said unto him, Abraham is our father. Jesus saith unto them, If ye were Abraham's children, ye would do the works of Abraham. But now ye seek to kill me, a man that hath told you the truth, which I have heard of God: this did not Abraham.*
> John 8:38-40

PROPHETIC PRINCIPLE #57

The cross of Jesus Christ is the identification with the people that are victims of society.

It's only fair to warn you...there is a price for declaring the truth. You can be killed for telling the truth. Some folks will hate you and others will seek to supplant the truth by feeding you a lie. They'll tell you that you're overreacting—-you've twisted the Scriptures- color doesn't make a difference. The prehistoric anointing of ages past will loose a dinosaur of religiosity against you, and pterodactyls will be sent for your destruction. God wants you to embrace what He is saying in this hour, for this is an hour of change. God is raising up men and women that are going to begin to declare the Word of the Lord and bring liberation to those that need to hear this word. These will be men and women that will be prepared for martyrdom....the conviction of truth may lead to their demise...but the truth shall echo from their graves. The Word of the Lord shall not be silenced, but shall smash against the wall of opposition and erode the mandates of men that dare to defy the Most High.

John 8:41,
> *Ye do the deeds of your father. Then said they to him, We be not born of fornication; we have one Father even God.*

> **PROPHETIC PRINCIPLE #58**
>
> **Blacks have no business sitting under white leadership in the Church in this particular age.**

The image of God that reflects upon your skin is not a mistake. You are fearfully and wonderfully made. God said, in verse 43, "Why do ye not understand my speech? even because ye cannot hear my word." Even though we've shown you in the Scriptures that Jesus was a man of color, yet you still don't understand my speech and you say, "Let me hold on to the white Jesus."

I've had an individual tell me, "We're not ready for a black Jesus." I reminded him what the Scripture said. He stated, "We know what the Scripture says, but we're not ready." That, to me, is frightening, coming from a born again, tongue speaking individual. Someone else indicated, "Prophet, how can you preach a message like this when you see the state that the people are in? Maybe you need to preach another message." I said, "No, I must continue to preach truth. I stand before God, and have a responsibility to speak what He is saying. If I am disobedient, He will no doubt say to me, I have given you the illumination of My Word in this matter; why did you hold your peace concerning it?

The ministry and the work of the prophet is not just telling you that a check is coming in the mail in about three days or letting you know about that promotion that's just around the corner. The prophetic ministry has become somewhat glamorized. But the prophet must speak the unpopular message that goes against the norm, for the natural tendency of people is to follow the path of least resistance. When God gets ready to speak to the sins of a nation, His mouthpieces must speak what He is saying, and not what the people want to hear. They must stand toe to toe with the oppressor and say, "Let my people go."

PROPHETIC PRINCIPLE #59

When you start in error you continue in error.

> ... He was a murderer from the beginning, and abode not in the truth, because there is no truth in him. When he speaketh a lie, he speaketh of his own: for he is a liar, and the father of it. And because I tell you the truth, ye believe me not.
> John 8:44-45

Many of you who have been brainwashed will have to read this book over and over and over again. You have been subject to years of programming which is contrary to the nature and the Word of God. So, when you hear truth, you fight it and call it a lie. Our greatest opposition is not with our oppressors - which is to be expected - but rather, it is from our own who have been brainwashed, and believe that God has called them to become color-blind. Our most vicious indictments come from individuals that have lost their connection with their identity. When you remove a tree from its roots, it is dead, and we are wrestling with dead "trees." When roots are removed from the earth, it will not live. Your future is over if you're not connected to your roots. Knowing your genealogy is important because once you know from whence you came, you'll know where you're going.

PROPHETIC PRINCIPLE #60

Kingdom mentality encompasses real estate.

The Jews will not let you forget their past. They will remind you of their Holocaust. Repeatedly. They will continue to write books and make movies about the Holocaust from now until Jesus comes. They will keep their pain before the eyes of the world continually. Where are the movie-makers that will unveil our Holocaust? We lost more in our Holocaust than they did, yet we have born again Christians who feel "that's not necessary." Well, people that forget their past are doomed to repeat it. To forget the past experiences and sufferings is unscriptural, for what was Jesus celebrating at the Last Supper? Why are the bitter herbs a part of the Passover meal? Denying your history makes you a part of the genocide. You will be part of the reason why "reservations" shall appear in America again.

I want to share a document I found by David J. Basch, a South African theologian teacher of the University of South Africa. He wrote the following in a Journal of Religious Studies some 200 years ago:

PROPHETIC PRINCIPLE #61

If you are of God, you will love the Truth

"As far as the Continent of Africa is concerned, black theology was born some 270 years ago near the mouth of the Congo River in present day Angola. In about the year 1700, a Congolese girl, Kempervita with the baptismal name of Beatrice, began appearing in public as a prophetess. She claimed to have had several visions and to have experienced death and resurrection. She said that St. Anthony had taken possession of her and had commanded her to preach and teach. She, like St. Francis of Assisi, first gave away all of her possessions. She then launched a protest movement against the Roman Catholic church. She forbade her followers to keep the times of fasting, to participate in many church ceremonies and to sing the Ave Maria and the Salve Novena. She probably did so because she saw these practices as meaningless, parrot-like expressions of Christianity. Crosses and crucifix' had to be destroyed as they were nothing but new fetishes which had replaced the old ones. Of greater importance, however, is the fact that Beatrice taught that Christ appeared as a black man in Salvador and that all His apostles were black. He was a Christ who identified Himself with the African who threw in His lot of that with the suffering, oppressed blacks, as opposed to white exploiters and oppressors. Therefore, Christ would, according to her teachings, restore the old Congolese kingdom and establish a Paradise on earth."

You start getting in trouble when you become Kingdom minded. When you tell people "The Rapture is cancelled," "Unpack your bags," "We're not going up until we grow up" - (Mind you, I'm not saying Jesus isn't coming, for He's coming back, but the way He's coming back is not the way you've been taught), you touch a sacred cow that will charge you in its pain.

"Beatrice's public ministry lasted for only a short period."

Your ministry will only last for a short period when you start speaking truth. However, be glad to know that you can move in an area of faith because they can't take your life. They'll have to wait for you to lay it down. "Like Joan of Arc, she died at the stake with the Name of Jesus upon her lips ..."

> **PROPHETIC PRINCIPLE #62**
>
> **Until you are walking in your Christianity and forsake the trivial glamor of being "born again" that has been nurtured in this society, you will not be able to pick up the cross of Jesus.**

In every generation, I believe God hand picked men and women to carry the message but something showed up to put the fire out. I want you to know that in this generation this fire is going to burn, for He's not speaking this message through one man or one woman. He's speaking this message through a body of people. It's a new day!

In this hour, we will begin to wake up as to who we are, and will begin to understand that Jesus meant for us to walk in the liberty wherewith He has made us free. We are a viable part of the Kingdom of God. The Kingdom is not only spiritual but a total revolution of the structure of the old world system. The Kingdom of God will bring conflict when you begin to understand it.

> **PROPHETIC PRINCIPLE #63**
>
> **When you start embracing the principles of the Kingdom, your lifestyle must change.**

The cross of Jesus, in this hour, represents the suffering in an unjust society. People will point out that there are white members who are a part of my church, and that there are some who have left during the discourse of this message. Why? Because they were like Orpah. They went along as long as their egos were satiated with the feeling of superiority. They liked the stage of dating, where they could be stroked and caressed and mingle with a tingle. But when it came time for the painful commitment to identify with the oppression of a people in pain, they became as Orpah, and had to return to their own people. They could not embrace our identity as Ruth did Naomi. They could not forsake the ways of their forefathers, nor did they wish to confront the responsibility of generational sin. They could not say "Your God is my God, and your people shall be my people. Where you go, I will go and where you dwell there will I dwell. Where you die, I will die and there will I be buried." The point of disconnection came at the junction of identification. When we started talking about the oppressor and about racism, they said, "See ya! Don't wanna be ya!"

The cross of Jesus Christ is the identification with the people that are victims of society. It is the affiliation with those that are oppressed. When the Romans gave the believers the name "Christians," they were mocking them; they said they were "Christ-like." How much more of a mockery would it be if they say, "You are identifying with the One who looks as if they were burned in the furnace." Christ-like. "You became a lover of that type of people?" Christ-like. "You are identifying with the suffering of what we may consider the scum of the earth?" Christ-like. Until you are walking in your Christianity and forsake the trivial glamor of being "born again" that has been nurtured in this society, you will not be able to pick up the cross of Jesus.

When you start embracing the principles of the Kingdom, your lifestyle must change. The resurrection is the experience of liberation, not only for Jesus but in every instance where elements of oppression are overcome and new life begins to break forth.

> **PROPHETIC PRINCIPLE #64**
>
> ## Success is easy to attain but difficult to maintain.

I was negotiating at a trade show and a white male addressed us as we were leaving and said, "Okay, boys, see you later." I said, "Excuse me, it's men." When I returned the next day, the insult continued. "How you boys doing today?" Now, he said "boys" one time too many! We had to stop and give him a lesson on why he could not call us "boys," and told him that some years ago, white men like himself would call grown black men boys but they, in turn, were bound by law to address a 12 year old boy as Master Bob. There were 70,000 whites represented at the trade show, and we couldn't find 200 blacks present because white men, like him, still see us as boys. We pointed out to him that he didn't come to do business with us as men. We made such a scene until one of the individuals that was with us spoke with the head of the company, and informed him of what was happening. There we were, ready to spend tens of thousands of dollars on some equipment,

> **PROPHETIC PRINCIPLE #65**
>
> **Liberation will always bring disgust to those who've held you captive.**

and we were suffering the insult of being called boys. The person in charge was shocked and called the salesman over asking, "Since when do we call our clients "boys"? Thank God, he was a Spirit-filled, tongue-talking believer that would not side with the oppressor. I must report here, that the oppressor was told who he should see, give the time he'd been there and was told to pick up his check the following week. Yes, he was fired!

I want you to know that we're still dealing with a spirit of this age. "Are you against whites?" No, but I am against that "white" mindset that sees and views themselves as superior and sees blacks as inferior. That's the spirit that we're up against, the spirit that I must fight against, and the spirit that God is going to destroy.

Let me tell you...in corporate America, men are working on jobs are seen as boys, and are still being offered a boy's salary. They'll even tell you that you should be happy. "Be a nice boy. You'll grow up in this company one day." If the Church is going to usher in the Kingdom, everyone must know that the Church must demand liberation, both spiritual and political, for liberation cannot be maintained without wealth. Success is easy to attain but you need something more to maintain.

> **PROPHETIC PRINCIPLE #66**
>
> **Liberation will come whether men like it or not.**

The Bible documents its favor for those who must function outside of the power of society. Look at what God did with Joseph. In this hour, God is raising up a "Joseph Company." Men who were sold into slavery by their brethren. Yet somehow, God is bringing elevation, and they shall sit in the seat of the palace.

The Word of the Lord in this hour is that this nation shall experience his dilemma but God had Joseph in a place of readiness. The Bible says in Psalms - "He shall teach his senators wisdom." We, as believers, must refuse victimization and minister to the victim. Some people say, "It sounds like you're preaching violence." No, we're talking self-defense.

The Word of the Lord is the active engagement of God bringing about what He has proclaimed that He will do. God said He will liberate us and the Word of the Lord has come that it's our time. God is driving forward what is behind. He is in the process of expressing that which He has declared to be so.

Liberation will always bring disgust to those who have held you captive. Everyone will not be excited about this message. Some will ask for forgiveness but hear me, the way of forgiveness is through reparation. The Bible calls it "restitution." "Restitution" means they have to restore the 300 years that we were robbed and enslaved and bring us up to the level we are supposed to be. We should be given the compensation for the wages we were never paid, and be compensated for the areas we were denied.

> **PROPHETIC PRINCIPLE #67**
>
> **God's future acts will not contradict God's former acts.**

It's amazing that everyone thought it so noble that a President wanted to give every American 40 acres and the mule. Who wants a mule? It's sterile, just like many of the empty promises and statements that have been espoused by bleeding heart liberals. We should have known that promise wasn't of God—- whenever God gives you something, He gives you something with seed in it.

God's future acts will not contradict God's former acts. God will drown your enemy in that which He brings you through. His will is irresistible. Liberation will come whether men like it or not. Liberation gives to human beings the enjoyment of the freedom of movement and the ability of self-determination. Liberation goes beyond the physical into the spiritual for the human spirit has been designed to soar. When we get the chains off your mind, you're going to soar. There's something super about us, that's why they've tried to reduce us from supermen to subhuman men.

Africa was a land of the spirit. Africans don't need to be taught anything about the supernatural, because they live in that realm. You don't have to go to an African and teach them to believe in God. You won't hear them saying, "I don't believe in God." We have always known the existence of God.

Cultural liberation from the limitations of prejudiced men will bring freedom from negative self images. It will stop us from a associating blackness with sin. It will stop us from associating white with purity and honesty. For where Jesus is, that is where the church is to be found. God will be found where men are enslaved because Jesus is found suffering with the suffering. So, if you're going to pick up the cross of Jesus in this hour, you will be found suffering with the suffering - Whatever color or race you are. God desires to make you free!

VIDEO CASSETTES
BY BISHOP E. BERNARD JORDAN

RACIAL ETHICS OF THE KINGDOM
Confronts the intrinsic racism that has permeated Christian doctrine. A Thorough study of the "traditional" teachings of the Church unveils a deliberate strain of racism that fosters white supremacy and eradicates the image of God within the African-American. It was this same strain of religiosity that soothed the consciousness of many and justified the atrocities of slavery in America. This series delineates the patent effects of such doctrine and restores the dignity of all races under God that were created for His divine purpose. 4-Video series $80

FREEDOM: THE WAY OF LIBERATION
A clarification of God's true definition of freedom and the resulting implications of the facade of liberty that continues to enslave the African-American community. The continuous assault of malevolent imagery that society uses to deliberately cripple the function of an entire race of people and deface their cultural legacy actually recreates Jesus Christ, the anointed Deliver of men, into an effigy that is crucified afresh on a daily basis. True freedom will emerge as the traditions of men are dethroned and replaced by the uncompromising Word of God that will cut every insidious lie asunder. This series will offend many who have been blinded by the hypnotic lies that have lulled their purpose to sleep, and challenge others to look beyond the veil of mediocrity and prejudice and behold the beauty of God's original intention towards men. This four-tape series is an unforgettable encounter with past, present and future as it proclaims the manifest destiny of the African-American and the Kingdom of God. 4-Video series $80

A PASSAGE TO LIBERATION
"A Passage to Liberation" is a thought-provoking edict against the dichotomy of society's offer of "Liberation" towards the African-American, versus their true liberty as ordained by God. The ingrained levels of prejudice that are encountered on a daily basis are indicated through the ethical teachings of the Word of God. Your spirit will be stirred to defy the implied boundaries of racial denigration, and thrust into the zenith of your capabilities through Jesus Christ. 4-Video series $80

PREPARATION FOR LEADERSHIP
A scathing indictment upon the insidious racism that permeates American society. Using Exodus Chapter 2 as his premise, Bishop Jordan delivers a powerful comparison between the pattern of oppressive leadership that requires divine intervention in the affairs of men and culminated in the appointment of Moses as the deliverer of Israel with the oppressive leadership that the African-American encounters within society and within the walls of the Church. Frightening in its accuracy, this teaching, though disturbing to the ear, is truly the Word of the Lord for this hour, for there are serious ramifications that the Church must contend with if she is to bring a solution to the crisis of woe in this nation.
4-Video series $80

THE SPIRIT OF THE OPPRESSOR

This series, The Spirit of the Oppressor, by Bishop E. Bernard Jordan, attacks the very fiber of societal influence that manipulates the gospel to justify racial supremacy. The insidious attitudes that permeate the Church are also addressed, for judgment begins in the House of God. By understanding that the Church is called to be the example for the world to follow, this series is powerful in its ability to expose the evil that lurks in the shadows of the "acceptable norm," and echoes a clarion call for deliverance from the lie that masquerades as the truth. Are you REALLY ready for the Word of the Lord?
4-Video series .... $80 also available as a book.

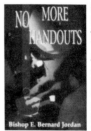
NO MORE HANDOUTS

In this series, Bishop E. Bernard Jordan addresses an inflammatory issue that has been instilled as a mindset within an entire nation of people. The American society has methodically caused generations of African-Americans to become dependent to a system that keeps them in a cycle of expectation that the government will always be their source of blessing. Bishop Jordan delineates the intention of God to bring prosperity to His people, thus charging them to turn their attention from the governmental system and discover the treasure that God has placed in their hands, for God is to be their source! This series is challenging and will force you to use your God-given abilities to thing creatively and generate wealth. You don't need anyone's permission to increase, for God has already decreed that you would multiply and wax exceedingly mighty!! This radical message is for a radical people!!
4-Video series $80

THE CROSSING

Bishop E. Bernard Jordan delivers a powerful teaching that defines the attitude that one must take as they begin to cross over their Jordan into the promised land. The paradigms of the old must be shattered as the image of change comes into view. One cannot embrace a new day loaded with old apparatus that is inoperative; old concepts that only brought you to a place of desperation and frustration. Rather, one must search the Word of God and renew your mind to Kingdom thinking that will bring elevation into your life. This series will sweep the cobwebs of mediocrity out of your life, and provoke you to a higher plane of right thinking that will thrust you into the path of dreams fulfilled. Straightforward in his approach, Bishop Jordan preaches a message that is inflammatory to the lies that have taken residence in your mind, and instills the purity of truth that is the nature of Almighty God. 4-Video series $80

UNDRESSING THE LIE

In this series, Bishop E. Bernard Jordan addresses a crucial issue in the Body of Christ -- RACISM. This series will captivate those who are true lovers of truth, for Jesus Christ is the Truth, and many have hidden Him and His cultural reality from the eyes of many. By conducting a thorough search of the Scriptures, Bishop Jordan identifies the Bible's description of Jesus that has been marred by the lies of those who wished to destroy an entire nation's concept of themselves, instead rendering theology that warped the image of God and denigrated them by teaching that they were cursed. Questions that have wandering in the minds of many for hundreds of years are answered as Bishop Jordan takes a strong stand to unmask the lies that have been masquerading as Truth. 4-Video series $80

LEGACY
In this series, Bishop E. Bernard Jordan expounds upon the African presence within the Scriptures. Combatting the misnomers that Africans were cursed by God and that they had very little to do with the unfolding of Biblical events, Bishop Jordan smashes the veil of delusion to cause the obvious truth to surface. During this season, God is causing a cultural renaissance to emerge. The oppressor of American society has lulled the minds of most people into a stupor of ignorance leaving them landless, powerless, and, once again, easy to enslave. The historical accounts within the Scriptures have been bequeathed as a legacy from our ancestors to proclaim the Word of the Lord against the sophisticated genocide that is affecting the African-American. A nation that ignores its past is doomed to repeat its failures in the future. Bishop Jordan brings clarity and balance to an inflammatory topic that is frequently misunderstood. 4-Video series $80

ECONOMICS: THE PATH TO EMPOWERMENT
This vital tape series by Bishop E. Bernard Jordan and Prophet Robert Brown deals with God's answers to the financial instability that has crippled the strength of the African-American nation. By defining the true motivation behind the onslaught of racism, Bishop Jordan and Prophet Brown give clear answers to the persistent societal obstacles that prevent most people from obtaining the true manifestation of God's intention for prosperity in their lives. The articulate questions that proceed from the heart of the nation shall be answered through the accumulation of wealth, for money shall answer all things. This teaching will expose the subtle racism that affects your financial future, and will provoke you into a mindset that will see obstacles as opportunities so that the full potential of God within you may express in your success!
2-Video series $40

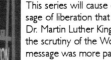

NO LIBERATION WITHOUT VIOLENCE
This series will cause one to Scripturally discern the validity of the message of liberation that echoed through America during the 60's through Dr. Martin Luther King and Malcolm X. By holding their messages up to the scrutiny of the Word of God, one cannot help but conclude whose message was more palatable to society, versus the message that stood in the integrity of the Scripture. Challenging in its content, this series is designed to attack the shackles of passivity and charge you to recognize the brutal realities of today's society. You are called to understand the true liberty of the gospel that Jesus preached. 4-Video series $80

A NEW GENERATION
Bishop E. Bernard Jordan is at his best in this series which portrays the change in one's attitude that must take place in order to attain your maximum potential in God and proceed to your Canaan Land! Like Joshua, one must be ready to be strong and of a good courage as you confront racism in this day. This is a radical message to eradicate error and bring forth the truth! Cutting in its intensity, this series will show you how the Word of the Lord will render you untouchable when you are aware of your purpose!! Bishop Jordan defines the new breed of people that God is raising up that will know the art of war, understand and love their enemy as they embrace the arms of destiny fulfilled.
4-Video series $80

ORDER FORM

ZOE MINISTRIES
4702 FARRAGUT ROAD • BROOKLYN, NY 11203 • (718) 282-2014

TITLE	QTY	DONATION	TOTAL

Subtotal	
Shipping	
Donation	
TOTAL	

Guarantee: You may return any defective item within 90 days for replacement. All offers are subject to change without notice. Please allow 4 weeks for delivery. No COD orders accepted. Make checks payable to ZOE MINISTRIES.

Name: _____ Phone _____

Address: _____

_____ Zip _____

Payment by: Check or Money Order (Payable to Zoe Ministries)
Visa • MasterCard • American Express • Discover

Card No.: _____ Exp. Date) _____

Signature (Required) _____